Round and Round the Mulberry Bush

by Jean Lenox Toddie

A SAMUEL FRENCH ACTING EDITION

NEW YORK HOLLYWOOD LONDON TORONTO

SAMUELFRENCH.COM

Copyright © 2010 by Jean Lenox Toddie

ALL RIGHTS RESERVED

CAUTION: Professionals and amateurs are hereby warned that *ROUND AND ROUND THE MULBERRY BUSH* is subject to a Licensing Fee. It is fully protected under the copyright laws of the United States of America, the British Commonwealth, including Canada, and all other countries of the Copyright Union. All rights, including professional, amateur, motion picture, recitation, lecturing, public reading, radio broadcasting, television and the rights of translation into foreign languages are strictly reserved. In its present form the play is dedicated to the reading public only.

The amateur and professional live stage performance rights to *ROUND AND ROUND THE MULBERRY BUSH* are controlled exclusively by Samuel French, Inc., and licensing arrangements and performance licenses must be secured well in advance of presentation. PLEASE NOTE that amateur Licensing Fees are set upon application in accordance with your producing circumstances. When applying for a licensing quotation and a performance license please give us the number of performances intended, dates of production, your seating capacity and admission fee. Licensing Fees are payable one week before the opening performance of the play to Samuel French, Inc., at 45 W. 25th Street, New York, NY 10010.

Licensing Fee of the required amount must be paid whether the play is presented for charity or gain and whether or not admission is charged.

Stock/professional licensing fees quoted upon application to Samuel French, Inc.

For all other rights than those stipulated above, apply to: Samuel French, Inc., 45 West 25th Street, New York, NY 10010.

Particular emphasis is laid on the question of amateur or professional readings, permission and terms for which must be secured in writing from Samuel French, Inc.

Copying from this book in whole or in part is strictly forbidden by law, and the right of performance is not transferable.

Whenever the play is produced the following notice must appear on all programs, printing and advertising for the play: "Produced by special arrangement with Samuel French, Inc."

Due authorship credit must be given on all programs, printing and advertising for the play.

ISBN 978-0-573-60121-7   Printed in U.S.A.   #29712

No one shall commit or authorize any act or omission by which the copyright of, or the right to copyright, this play may be impaired.

No one shall make any changes in this play for the purpose of production.

Publication of this play does not imply availability for performance. Both amateurs and professionals considering a production are strongly advised in their own interests to apply to Samuel French, Inc., for written permission before starting rehearsals, advertising, or booking a theatre.

No part of this book may be reproduced, stored in a retrieval system, or transmitted in any form, by any means, now known or yet to be invented, including mechanical, electronic, photocopying, recording, videotaping, or otherwise, without the prior written permission of the publisher.

MUSIC USE NOTE

Licensees are solely responsible for obtaining formal written permission from copyright owners to use copyrighted music in the performance of this play and are strongly cautioned to do so. If no such permission is obtained by the licensee, then the licensee must use only original music that the licensee owns and controls. Licensees are solely responsible and liable for all music clearances and shall indemnify the copyright owners of the play and their licensing agent, Samuel French, Inc., against any costs, expenses, losses and liabilities arising from the use of music by licensees.

IMPORTANT BILLING AND CREDIT REQUIREMENTS

All producers of *ROUND AND ROUND THE MULBERRY BUSH* *must* give credit to the Author of the Play in all programs distributed in connection with performances of the Play, and in all instances in which the title of the Play appears for the purposes of advertising, publicizing or otherwise exploiting the Play and/or a production. The name of the Author *must* appear on a separate line on which no other name appears, immediately following the title and *must* appear in size of type not less than fifty percent of the size of the title type.

CONTENTS

Did You Hear the Owl Last Night?..........................7
Once Again in Glyn Kerrie..............................45

DID YOU HEAR THE OWL LAST NIGHT?

A DRAMATIC COMEDY IN ONE ACT

CHARACTERS

LEIGHTON – A professor of Philosophy in his late fifties.
THE OLD POOP – An elderly gardener.
HARRIET – A professor of English in her mid-forties.
STAR – A young girl age thirteen.
AUDREY – A college student.
VERONICA – An elderly teacher of Violin and Voice.

SCENE

A park in a small college town.

TIME

The present.

(*AT RISE: Slightly right of centerstage sits a bright green park bench. A cardboard cut-out of a six foot large bush sits stage right. Upstage left is a green wooden coat rack on which hang a dark woolen cap, a misshapen straw hat and faded yellow peaked hat. Also hanging on the rack are large cardboard cutouts of a green leaf, an orange leaf and a bright pink flower.*)

(*As the play opens* **THE OLD POOP** *shuffles on stage left. He moves to the coat rack, dons the woolen cap, picks up the cutout of the green leaf and shuffling stage right attaches it to the bush.*)

THE OLD POOP. (*to the bush in an age-roughened voice.*) You hear the owl last night? Some say when that ole bird screech gonna be a change in the weather. Gonna be change a-comin' when that ole bird he screech. (*mimes clipping branches*) Winter were cold as the devil's breath, weren't it? Devil whisperin' weren't gonna be no spring. But that ole bird knew that deep down yer roots was warmin." He knew. (*turns again to clipping*)

(**LEIGHTON** *appears stage left wearing a fine camel hair top coat marred by several moth holes, dark tan trousers, and carries a large tote bag. He speaks to the audience.*)

LEIGHTON. It's rumored I am to be found sitting here in the park most days. Some say I left the Halls of Ivy to become a ragged old professor in a moth eaten coat with newspaper in his shoes. Quite true. The soles of my shoes are thin, and newspaper protects my feet from the damp. As for my coat, one does not throw out a serviceable coat. No, no... (*smooths a hand along a sleeve*) This coat is fine wool. My great-great grandfather wore this coat during the dark days of the depression. Fortunately it was stored in the attic. Unfortunately I'd forgotten to put moth balls in the bag.

THE OLD POOP. *(turning to* **LEIGHTON***)* Mornin' sir.

LEIGHTON. Ah, good morning.

THE OLD POOP. *(resumes clipping)* Did you hear that ole owl last night?

LEIGHTON. No, I don't believe I did.

THE OLD POOP. There's them that says when the ole bird he hoot many a life is gonna change.

LEIGHTON. Is that right?

THE OLD POOP. Aye. Some say that ole bird he wise.

LEIGHTON. I've heard that said.

THE OLD POOP. Some say that ole bird he foolish.

LEIGHTON. Oh? What do you say?

THE OLD POOP. I say change is a-comin' an' we best be ready. *(nods ominously, resumes clipping)*

LEIGHTON. Nothing can dampen my spirits on such a day. *(turns to the audience)* And as for the rumor that I'm performing miracles? A ragged old duffer with newspaper in his shoes performing miracles? Ridiculous. No, no. I collect miracles. When I leave home in the morning my pockets are empty. By dusk these pockets are full. *(Stretching out his arms, he breathes deeply.)* "T's spring," the poets sing. *(does a little dance step)* And time is mine to while away. Soon azaleas will be in bloom. There will be blossoms on the weeping cherry.

THE OLD POOP. When that ole black bird he hoots et's a warnin'. Some fish'll take the hook. Some fish won't.

LEIGHTON. Ah, questions. While at the university I sat at the kitchen table in the evening sipping black tea through a sugar cube and pondering questions asked by saints and sinners, burghers and beggars since time began.

THE OLD POOP. Questions eat at one come dark.

LEIGHTON. But now when sipping black tea through a sugar cube I lay miracles out on the kitchen table and ponder for whom each is meant. In truth I am a peddler of miracles. *(sits on the bench)*

THE OLD POOP. Never met up with one of them miracles.

LEIGHTON. You're looking at one. Your bushes are blossoming.

(He digs into his tote bag removes a bag of red grapes, pops one into his mouth.)

(HARRIET enters stage left. A comely woman in her late forties with good legs she wears an deep aquamarine coat and carries a leather case.)

HARRIET. Leighton?

LEIGHTON. Harriet! You find me here sitting in the sun enjoying a few grapes. Will you join me?

HARRIET. I hardly recognized you! You look ghastly!

LEIGHTON. You look well.

(Turns, speaks softly to an unseen someone sitting beside him on the bench.)

Yes, dear, if you wish. Yes, of course. Do be careful.

(turns back to HARRIET)

Join me?

HARRIET. No, no.

LEIGHTON. You have an appointment?

HARRIET. Places to go, things to do… *(Starts stage right. Stops.)* Leighton, that coat!

LEIGHTON. Moth eaten, but serviceable.

HARRIET. Who were you talking to?

LEIGHTON. My wife.

HARRIET. Jennifer?

LEIGHTON. Yes.

HARRIET. Are you mad? I was at her funeral!

LEIGHTON. That distressed her.

HARRIET. Distressed her?

LEIGHTON. She was not fond of you.

HARRIET. I was well aware. But why?

LEIGHTON. Because I was.

HARRIET. You were a rascal.

LEIGHTON. And you were a flirt. *(pats the bench)* Come flirt with me.

HARRIET. Leighton, I've grown up as you've grown old. I'll not be taken in by your blarney.

LEIGHTON. Shucks.

HARRIET. And those bagpipes!

LEIGHTON. At the funeral?

HARRIET. Yes. I don't like bagpipes.

LEIGHTON. Perhaps that's why she wished to have them.

HARRIET. You're quite mad. Talking to a woman who is...

LEIGHTON. Deceased? Yes. Dear Jennifer is deceased, but at times I feel her presence and seek her advice. She is quite amenable to you joining me.

HARRIET. She loathed me.

LEIGHTON. She no longer holds grudges. *(pats the bench)*

HARRIET. Oh! *(laughing, joins him on the bench)*

*(Finished with his clipping **THE OLD POOP** shuffles stage left.)*

LEIGHTON. My good man...

*(**THE OLD POOP** turns.)*

Harriet, I'd like you to meet the gentleman who tends these beautiful gardens.

HARRIET. The daffodils are lovely.

THE OLD POOP. Thank you, ma'am. *(shuffles stage left, exits)*

LEIGHTON. *(to **HARRIET**)* You're wearing the same scent.

HARRIET. Yes.

LEIGHTON. A scent redolent of memory.

HARRIET. I'm not the foolish girl I was.

LEIGHTON. Will you join me?

(He extends the bag of grapes. Throughout the play when offered grapes characters mime taking and eating them. She hesitates, takes one. He does as well. They simultaneously pop them in their mouths.)

HARRIET. Grandpa had a grape arbor.

LEIGHTON. Oh?

HARRIET. And Grandma was the last woman in the neighborhood to hang clothes on the line to bleach in the sun. *(leans back, closes her eyes for a moment)* Grandpa's long johns flapping in the breeze. Always nicely mended. And a coal stove in the kitchen. Grandpa polished it until it shone like a black diamond. Always a pot of sauce simmering. And Great-Grandmother rocking in the sun by the window, a clove of garlic around her neck to ward off evil spirits.

LEIGHTON. I hear it's efficacious.

HARRIET. Perhaps you should wear one. Honestly, Leighton, from tenured professor to welfare in the blink of an eye? Walking out of the university without so much as a fare-thee-well? Why?

LEIGHTON. It was a golden October afternoon. Red and amber leaves carpeted the campus. I was lecturing on the Muslim mystics when suddenly I realized I had said all I have to say.

HARRIET. The Dean was furious! Everyone was! Just tipped your hat and walked away!

LEIGHTON. I had always wakened at dawn, strapped on my armor and gone forth to fight the good fight against ignorance. But over time my knees grew weak and my armor rusted.

HARRIET. Rubbish!

LEIGHTON. I left to find something that would get me out of bed in the morning.

HARRIET. And did you?

LEIGHTON. Indeed.

HARRIET. What?

LEIGHTON. Grapes.

HARRIET. Oh, Leighton!

LEIGHTON. And lollypops.

HARRIET. I'm weary as well and my feet ache, but I'm still standing in front of students all day trying to teach them to think. Think for themselves, not hunch over the internet.

LEIGHTON. Tapped out, huh? I suggest you rap their knuckles, walk out and join me the bench. Otherwise, stop bitching.

HARRIET. You're horrid!

LEIGHTON. Don't tell.

HARRIET. I'm an educator! I've given irreplaceable years attempting to enlighten young minds. Now I sit through graduations wondering what have I wrought?

LEIGHTON. Take off your shoes.

HARRIET. Take off my shoes?

LEIGHTON. Feel the earth beneath your feet.

HARRIET. For heaven's sake, grow up! *(after a moment)* Oh, Why not! *(steps out of her shoes, stretches her legs)* I admit I'm tired, too.

LEIGHTON. Of teaching?

HARRIET. No, I love teaching. I'm tired I have nothing but teaching. Why am I living in that dreary apartment?

LEIGHTON. *(steps out of his shoes)* Dance with me.

(Drawing her to her feet he swings her around the bench singing the childhood song.)

"Here we go round the mulberry bush,
   The mulberry bush, the mulberry bush,
Here we go round the mulberry bush
   so early in the morning."

HARRIET. *(drops to the bench laughing)* What if your wife should see us?

LEIGHTON. She's a good sport. *(slips into his shoes, kneels to replace hers)* You say your grandfather had a grape arbor?

HARRIET. There are still a few grape arbors down on Roma Street.

LEIGHTON. Roma Street you say? How about that?

(searches in his tote bag, removes a newspaper clipping, reads it, tucks it in his pocket)

Do you have a garden, Harriet?

HARRIET. A few potted plants and a hamster I call Jacques, who doesn't talk back and also likes grapes.

LEIGHTON. They tell me a grape arbor needs tending

HARRIET. As a child I helped grandpa tend the arbor. It was so peaceful, Leighton. Nothing but the sound of bees buzzing and the scent of the fruit. I wish I were that child again.

LEIGHTON. May an old castaway give some advice?

HARRIET. Have I ever been able to stop you?

LEIGHTON. Harriet, my dear, for once in your life dare to be outrageous.

HARRIET. I wouldn't know how.

LEIGHTON. Dye your hair the color of marmalade.

HARRIET. Your wife dyed her hair the color of marmalade.

LEIGHTON. And she sang in the elevator.

HARRIET. She couldn't carry a tune.

LEIGHTON. Ask for five dollar bills when you cash your paycheck. Throw them out a window on the top floor of the Broad Street bank building.

HARRIET. And go hungry until my next paycheck.

LEIGHTON. Come share my Wheaties, then sit here on the bench with me.

HARRIET. And eat grapes?

LEIGHTON. When we tire of holding hands.

HARRIET. Your wife would not approve.

LEIGHTON. At least consider moving from that dreary apartment. Both potted plants and Jacque are portable.

HARRIET. But am I?

LEIGHTON. *(He offers her a grape, takes one himself, they simultaneously pop them in their mouths.)* So a grape arbor needs tending.

HARRIET. Tender tending.

LEIGHTON. We all need tender tending.

HARRIET. I used to help Grandpa on Saturday mornings.

LEIGHTON. A chore?

HARRIET. Chore? Oh, no. I've never felt as content. Neither Grandpa nor I needing to say anything. Both of us comfortable with the silence. Comfortable with each other in the heat of the noonday sun.

(STAR, wearing oversize overalls, enters stage left on a run. Skids to a stop.)

STAR. You seen 'im?

LEIGHTON. Who?

STAR. Him! *(runs off stage left)*

LEIGHTON. *(to HARRIET, imitating STAR)* You seen him?

HARRIET. *(playing along.)* Who?

LEIGHTON. Him!

(They chuckle, lean back in comfortable silence.)

LEIGHTON. Are you happy, Harriet?

HARRIET. I'm afraid to ask myself. *(after a moment)* No.

LEIGHTON. No, not happy, or, no, won't ask yourself?

HARRIET. Both or neither. But at the moment I'm happy sitting here in the sun with an old friend in a moth-eaten coat eating…what do you call these grapes?

LEIGHTON. I call them love bites.

HARRIET. May I have another?

LEIGHTON. As many as you wish.

HARRIET. One will do.

(He leans over, lifts her chin and kisses her lightly on the lips.)

That was uncalled for, but thank you.

(hiccups, begins to cry)

LEIGHTON. *(taking a handkerchief from his pocket, wipes her tears)* Few women are lovely when they weep. You are among the few.

HARRIET. Lovely? Oh, Leighton, I'm pathetic. A middle-age woman living alone with a rodent.

LEIGHTON. Just so. If only you weren't too old to tend a grape arbor.

HARRIET. Too old? Grandpa was eighty-six! He walked to the market every day, made wine in the basement, stirred the sauce and chased pretty women. At age eighty-six!

LEIGHTON. I would lift a glass to Grandpa if I had a glass to lift.

HARRIET. Many a glass of Grandpa's wine was lifted in that dear old, yellow kitchen.

LEIGHTON. Yellow?

HARRIET. Bright yellow. The color of Grandma's lemon pie. On sunny days Great-Grandma dozed in the rocking chair by the window dreaming of the old country.

LEIGHTON. A great-grandma smelling of garlic.

HARRIET. Everyone in Grandma's house smelled of garlic. It's where the neighbors gathered. No one knocked. Walked in the back door and hung out in Grandma's yellow kitchen, sunny even on the darkest days.

LEIGHTON. The picture you paint is pleasant, but what of Jacques and his penchant for fine French cheese. Would Jacques be content in a kitchen where a pot of Italian sauce simmers on the back burner?

HARRIET. Italians make delicious cheese. Once he tasted it…

LEIGHTON. He would prefer it? No, no, you've indoctrinated him. Jacques is French. Jacques is obstinate.

HARRIET. Would I have a hamster who couldn't think for himself?

LEIGHTON. Is he as ornery as you?

HARRIET. Would I have a hamster who isn't? *(Offered a grape, she shakes her head.)* It's pleasant sitting here in the sun.

(**VERONICA** *enters stage right wearing an ancient green gown under a cape and carrying a velvet drawstring purse. She stops, looks around, approaches* **LEIGHTON.**)

VERONICA. Perhaps you can help me. I do believe there is a diner in the area?

LEIGHTON. Indeed there is. Past the entrance to the park and down the street a few steps.

VERONICA. *(fumbles in her purse, withdraws a little ivory fan, fans her brow)* It's warmer than I thought. It does take the pluck out of one. *(takes an uncertain step)*

HARRIET. *(rises)* Do sit down.

VERONICA. No, no, I shan't disturb you. No, I'm quite alright. I simply get a little flustered when I lose my way. When I was your age, young and lovely as you, I danced all night. The bell of the ball. Do continue your tête à tête. *(drifts stage left)* Charming, charming… the bell of the ball. *(exits)*

HARRIET. Poor old soul. And eating in a diner.

LEIGHTON. When she was your age she danced all night. I fear you don't even tap your toes.

HARRIET. I haven't the energy.

LEIGHTON. Harriet?

HARRIET. Umm?

LEIGHTON. Remember that afternoon?

HARRIET. That afternoon?

LEIGHTON. The afternoon we…

HARRIET. Leighton!

LEIGHTON. I've kissed many a beautiful woman, but none more passionate.

HARRIET. I am not a beautiful woman and have never been passionate about anyone or anything!

LEIGHTON. Except for Grandpa's grape arbor?

HARRIET. And Grandpa.

LEIGHTON. Fortunate fellow.

HARRIET. Shame on you. Talking this way when your wife is…where is she now down by the lake?

LEIGHTON. Oh, you see her too?

HARRIET. Of course I don't see her, but…

LEIGHTON. But…?

HARRIET. You were so bad you old coot! Imagine us all playing spin the bottle in the faculty lounge! The entire department was chastised!

LEIGHTON. Spin the bottle. Yum, yum.

HARRIET. Will you ever act your age?

LEIGHTON. I may frown now and then, but I shall never stop licking lollipops in the library. *(looks in the paper bag)* Not many left.

HARRIET. As a friend of mine would say, "shucks."

LEIGHTON. Out of the doldrums, dear girl?

HARRIET. I'm out of the doldrums, dear boy.

LEIGHTON. Splendid.

(THE OLD POOP enters stage left, scans the sky, turns to HARRIET.)

THE OLD POOP. Did you hear the owl last night?

HARRIET. No, but I sleep soundly. The owl is a bird of darkness they say.

THE OLD POOP. I ain't afeard of the dark…Time the spider spins a web to catch what's comin' and fairy folk dance on puddles. Got to spin me a web to catch that scallywag. *(tips his hat, exits stage right)*

HARRIET. He's a rare old fellow. *(to LEIGHTON)* As are you.

LEIGHTON. As a rare old fellow I, too, have a web to spin. *(reaches into his pocket, takes out a small newspaper clipping, passes it to her)*

HARRIET. *(reads it)* Real estate? *(thrusts it back to him)*

LEIGHTON. Jacques might enjoy a back yard. You might as well.

HARRIET. At my age?

LEIGHTON. Grandpa squashed grapes with his bare feet in the basement at age eighty-six. And doesn't the clipping mention an iron stove?

HARRIET. No.

LEIGHTON. Nothing is perfect. Even some grapes have pits.

HARRIET. You're suggesting I retire, put newspaper in my shoes to protect my feet from the damp and tend a grape arbor?

LEIGHTON. Don't you wish to retire?

HARRIET. No.

LEIGHTON. You just wish to sit here and grouse.

HARRIET. Yes. *(rising)* I must go.

LEIGHTON. Just a moment. *(rises, tucks the ad in her coat pocket)*

HARRIET. *(shaking her head)* Take care you crazy old coot. *(starts stage right)*

LEIGHTON. *(pops another grape in his mouth)* This grape has a pit!

HARRIET. Serves you right. *(exits)*

*(**LEIGHTON** stretches, smiles. Takes several pieces of paper from his pocket, studies them as **STAR** rushes on stage and skids to a stop. Scans the stage angrily, stamps her foot.)*

STAR. The old goat! Where's he got to?

*(turns, sees **LEIGHTON** sitting on the bench)*

Another old gaffer!

(runs to peer off stage left)

Shoot! *(stamps her foot)* He got me goin' crazy!

*(sees **LEIGHTON** watching her)*

Shove off!

LEIGHTON. Pardon?

STAR. I'm not some peep show! Shove off!

LEIGHTON. Why should I shove off?

STAR. 'Cause I need t' sit down!

  (**LEIGHTON** *pats the bench beside him.*)

  Alone!

LEIGHTON. Alone?

STAR. Like no one around!

LEIGHTON. The park is for everyone, child.

STAR. Look, I'm gettin' nervy.

LEIGHTON. Nervy?

STAR. I got me the jitters. You never had the jitters?

LEIGHTON. Not of late. Sit down, my dear.

STAR. I gotta spell it out? I need a smoke. Like I'm gonna park here an' blow smoke into some old geezer's nose? Smoke's not good for old geezers, an' I got my principles!

LEIGHTON. You're too young to smoke.

STAR. Never been young. Never had time. So shove off.

LEIGHTON. When I've just made the acquaintance of a young lady with principles?

STAR. Not young an' no lady.

LEIGHTON. *(holding out the bag)* Have a grape.

STAR. You tryin' t' letch me?

LEIGHTON. Certainly not. I, too, have my principles. These grapes are delicious. They're from Brazil.

STAR. So?

LEIGHTON. So sit down and enjoy a few.

STAR. You tryin' t' boss me?

LEIGHTON. Yes, tell me if I'm succeeding.

STAR. Geez! *(drops to the bench)* Look, old man, try somethin' an' you got trouble.

  (combs her hair off her face with her fingers)

  Hand me one of them grapes.

LEIGHTON. *(offering her a grape)* All the way from Brazil.

STAR. *(pops a grape into her mouth)* From Brats-ville, huh? My kinda grape 'cause I'm a brat. Born a brat an' be a brat till I hang. That's what teachers say.

LEIGHTON. Aren't these grapes delectable.

STAR. They're ok.

LEIGHTON. Would you like another?

(She takes another. He laughs.)

STAR. What's so funny?

LEIGHTON. Grapes from Brats-ville.

STAR. You comin' on t' me? I'm not sittin' here with some old letch comin' on t' me! I got my…

LEIGHTON. Principles.

STAR. Yeah!

LEIGHTON. I, too, have principles. I only allow myself to… letch…ladies who take their teeth out at night. Only such a lady can sing the song of life with me.

STAR. *(slides to the ground to retie a sneaker)* My mama could sing better than them old ladies that take their teeth out.

LEIGHTON. You haven't heard them sing.

STAR. Don't matter. No one could sing like my mama.

LEIGHTON. Oh?

STAR. An' she give me the gift. That's what my grandpa say. He say, "Your mama give you the gift." *(wraps her arms around her knees and sings softly the old lullaby, "Rock-a-by baby.")* I remember her singin' that.

LEIGHTON. Remember?

STAR. Yeah.

LEIGHTON. Your mother is…

STAR. Dead. Like drop dead. *(Her voice cracks.)* My mama dropped dead. Like Grandpa say, that's life.

(They sit in silence. Finally…)

You seen 'im?

LEIGHTON. Seen who?

STAR. The old poop.

LEIGHTON. The old…poop?

STAR. My grandpa.

LEIGHTON. I don't know that I've seen him.

STAR. You seen 'im you'd know. He takes off an' I gotta haul 'im in! I go an' get us a hunk of Portugese sausage an' now I can't find hide nor hair of 'im.

LEIGHTON. Your grandfather is Portuguese?

STAR. No, he's a gardener. Cuts grass, fertilizes, waters, dead heads the flowers. All such crap. You see 'im you tell 'im dead head is lookin' for 'im. That's what he calls me, dead head. You tell 'im dead head's gettin' pissed. Got it?

LEIGHTON. Let me see. Yes, I believe I've got it. If I should happen to see the old…poop I shall tell him that dead head is getting…pissed.

STAR. You can't call 'im an old poop!

LEIGHTON. Oh? Why is that?

STAR. 'Cause he's not your grandpa! He's my grandpa!

LEIGHTON. And that's your special name for him?

STAR. My special name, yeah! *(rises)* I got t' find 'im.

LEIGHTON. Perhaps we shall meet again.

STAR. You loopy?

LEIGHTON. I'm here about this time most every day. Suppose you were to pass by when you're feeling nervy and need to sit down. We might become friends.

STAR. Like that's gonna happen!

LEIGHTON. Just suppose. Would there be a chance I might become someone special? A chance I might become an…old poop?

STAR. No way!

LEIGHTON. I thought not. I don't believe I've ever been that special to anyone.

STAR. An' if I do walk by, you don't get to call me dead head neither.

LEIGHTON. I hadn't dared ask.

STAR. Only Grandpa gets t' call me that 'cause he's my own grandpa and he give me my principles. An' I buy 'im Portugese sausage when we gets the pennies. "When we get the pennies," he say, "we'll buy some Portugese sausage."

LEIGHTON. If I'm not to call you dead head then perhaps I should know your real name.

STAR. Why'd you wanna know my real name?

LEIGHTON. With me sitting in the park and you running through the park I'm sure we shall meet again and again.

STAR. Don't mean I'll stop t' talk an' only Mama and Grandpa knowed my real name an' I ain't tellin'!

LEIGHTON. Well now let me consider. Ah! I shall call you Star.

STAR. Star? Why'd you call me a goofy name like that?

LEIGHTON. Because with a little "spit and polish," and I just happen to have some here in my pocket, I predict some day my principled young lady you'll shine like a Star.

STAR. That'd be a miracle!

(**AUDREY** *enters stage right wearing jeans, a sweat shirt and carrying a back pack. She crosses to the bench, stands and stares at* **LEIGHTON.**)

AUDREY. You look as ratty as they say. Cool.

LEIGHTON. Ah, Audrey, child of light with mane of gold.

AUDREY. Hi. *(drops her backpack, squats on it)*

LEIGHTON. Shouldn't you be in class?

AUDREY. Shouldn't you?

LEIGHTON. No, child. I'm exactly where I should be.

AUDREY. So am I.

LEIGHTON. And where is that?

AUDREY. Sitting at your feet. *(gesturing toward* **STAR***)* You teaching grade school now?

LEIGHTON. I've forgotten my manners. May I introduce a friend. This young lady is Star. Star, this is a former student, Audrey.

AUDREY. *(rises)* Hi.

(STAR backs away.)

Hey, Huckleberry, I don't bite. And seeing as how the best professor at the university is teaching from a park bench now we might become fellow students. *(stretches out her hand)* Friends?

STAR. Cut the crap! *(runs off stage right)*

LEIGHTON. You've met your match.

AUDREY. I've yet to meet my match. But I doubt she'll invite me to her birthday party.

LEIGHTON. I doubt she's ever had a birthday party. I doubt she knows the month or the year.

AUDREY. She's hightailing it down the street.

LEIGHTON. Looking for the old poop.

AUDREY. Who?

LEIGHTON. That, Audrey, is Star's story. A story for her to tell.

AUDREY. Then I doubt I'll hear it.

(moves stage right to watch the fleeing child)

Spooky kid. *(turning)* Skuddlebut on campus says you're sick.

LEIGHTON. Oh?

AUDREY. Sick in the head.

LEIGHTON. I'm feeling quite chipper.

AUDREY. Having fun are you?

LEIGHTON. I giggle now and then.

AUDREY. Why's that kid so angry?

LEIGHTON. Why are you?

AUDREY. I'm not angry.

LEIGHTON. You're so angry your hair is on fire.

AUDREY. *(kicks her backpack)* I'm not the only one! The campus is a hotbed of hotheads since you left!

LEIGHTON. Would you like a grape?

AUDREY. No.

LEIGHTON. From Brazil. Quite tasty.

AUDREY. Like your little friend said, cut the crap.

LEIGHTON. How do I go about doing that?

AUDREY. Tell me why you walked out in the middle of a lecture?

LEIGHTON. *(studies her a moment)* I was an old man, Audrey, privileged to teach gifted students, you among them, when standing in the lecture hall one golden autumn afternoon I was suddenly aware my notes smelled of moth balls.

AUDREY. So once in awhile you repeated yourself. Some things are worth saying twice.

LEIGHTON. It's not that I said something I might have said before. It's that I had nothing new to say.

AUDREY. School sucks since you left.

LEIGHTON. Come now.

AUDREY. For someone like me.

LEIGHTON. Like you?

AUDREY. I want to be a writer. I'm tired of sitting on my ass taking notes.

LEIGHTON. Suffering from a tired tookis?

AUDREY. Don't patronize me, Professor Tyler!

LEIGHTON. I apologize. In my awkward way, Audrey, I'm trying to understand.

AUDREY. I've had my fill of listening to professors who've never walked back alleys at night tripping over mangy cats and kicking empty beer cans.

LEIGHTON. And you think I have? I'm in bed by ten and sleep like a baby.

AUDREY. Bullshit.

LEIGHTON. No.

AUDREY. Kids have seen you on the south side after midnight.

LEIGHTON. What were they doing on the south side at that hour?

AUDREY. What were you?

LEIGHTON. There are times I don't sleep like a baby. Times I like to walk dark streets looking for…

AUDREY. Dealers, ladies of the night?

LEIGHTON. Miracles.

AUDREY. Miracles? Well, if you find a few save one for me. I have a feeling I'll need it. *(lifts her backpack)* Without you the school's not worth a damn. *(exits stage left)*

LEIGHTON. We all need a miracle. Every one of us. We all need a miracle. *(checks his watch)* Tea time. Time for tea, and scones and a bit of Bach. Lovely time of day. *(exits stage left)*

(Brief silence. Music. Brief silence. The season is now summer.)

*(**THE OLD POOP** enters stage left, shuffles to the coat rack, replaces the woolen cap with the straw hat, takes the pink flower and attaches it to the bush. Wiping his forehead on his sleeve he speaks to the bush.)*

THE OLD POOP. Now ain't you all decked out? Pretty as the ladies at Sunday service. All pink and perfumed. *(stands back, admires the bush, stoops to loosen the soil)*

*(**LEIGHTON** enters stage left wearing a colorful Hawaiian shirt and carrying his tote bag.)*

Good morning.

THE OLD POOP. Mornin'.

LEIGHTON. Hot.

THE OLD POOP. July.

LEIGHTON. Umm. July.

THE OLD POOP. Need rain.

LEIGHTON. It's been awhile.

THE OLD POOP. Flowers is droopin'.

LEIGHTON. You're fond of flowers.

THE OLD POOP. *(rises)* Tended 'em many a year, plants an' posies, posies an' plants. All what's green and growin'.

VERONICA. *(from off stage right)* Mercy me!

THE OLD POOP. Somethin's up! *(hastens offstage)* Steady there! Here, take my arm! Hold on now. We'll go slow. No hurry, no hurry.

(VERONICA enters with the help of the old man. She wears her ancient green gown.)

VERONICA. I fear I was about to swoon. The heat...

LEIGHTON. *(jumps to his feet)* Oh, my!

(They help her to the bench.)

VERONICA. Thank you. So kind...so kind...

THE OLD POOP. Best set awhile. Summer does a body in.

VERONICA. I fear I don't dress appropriately.

THE OLD POOP. Settle yerself, ma'am. That's right. Rest a bit. I'd best see to my roses.

*(Tips his hat, nods to **LEIGHTON**, exits.)*

LEIGHTON. Should you be out in this heat?

VERONICA. I'd set my heart on dining in the diner down the street.

LEIGHTON. *(with a twinkle)* Does one "dine" when eating breakfast in a diner?

VERONICA. If it's one's birthday.

LEIGHTON. Today is your birthday?

VERONICA. To the best of my recollection.

LEIGHTON. Well, happy birthday.

VERONICA. Thank you. *(removes the fan from her purse, fans herself)* I do like diners.

LEIGHTON. As do I.

VERONICA. The smell of bacon fat and strong black coffee.

LEIGHTON. Ah.

VERONICA. The waitress calling out, "Hey George, how are you?" "Ok," George says. George is ok.

LEIGHTON. As are you now, I trust.

VERONICA. I've quite recovered, thank you. I've seldom been so flustered. Back in the diner I had what one might call a mystical experience. It quite took my breath away.

LEIGHTON. Oh?

VERONICA. I was enjoying a plate of pancakes and sausage when suddenly the diner and everyone in it began to glow.

LEIGHTON. Is that right?

VERONICA. The waitress, George, four men in hard hats cupping coffee mugs in their hands! Everyone was beautiful!

LEIGHTON. Oh, my.

VERONICA. Do you think they know how beautiful they are? Probably not. You probably have to be a ninety-one year-old woman sitting alone in the second booth from the rear on your birthday to see how beautiful everyone is. *(smooths her skirt)* My birthday gown.

LEIGHTON. The color suits you.

VERONICA. "Green, the color of life," a lover said. Or was it my husband? I can't recall.

LEIGHTON. One does lose track.

VERONICA. Makes no difference. But loss of memory does make a difference. It's fatiguing. Just this morning I was lying abed trying to recall the name of Godwin's second wife.

LEIGHTON. Godwin?

VERONICA. My husband. Or was he one of my lovers? No matter. All I can remember is that she was very fond of Eggs Benedict. *(fans her self, sighs)* I've worn this gown on my birthday for over sixty years.

LEIGHTON. Looking lovelier every year, I'm sure.

VERONICA. The first time I wore it was at a birthday luncheon in an outrageously expensive Parisian restaurant. *(closes her eyes, seems to drift off)*

LEIGHTON. Would you like a grape?

VERONICA. Oh dear, was I drifting off?

LEIGHTON. *(extending the bag)* Grapes. They're quite tasty.

VERONICA. Thank you. Oh, they are savory.

LEIGHTON. From Brazil.

VERONICA. Brazil? I adore Brazil. I sang Carmen in Brazil when I was young wearing this very gown.

LEIGHTON. I sense you are unaffected by the ebb and flow of fashion.

VERONICA. Quite right. I wear this same gown every year, now worn and frayed as I am.

LEIGHTON. Your visage outshines your gown, dear lady.

VERONICA. I delight in flattery, dear boy.

LEIGHTON. As do I when called a boy.

VERONICA. Why when I was not much younger than you the crown heads of Europe sought my company. And in Brazil my dressing room was overrun with suitors. Slender young men in tight black trousers with silky black mustaches.

LEIGHTON. Ah.

VERONICA. During the years of my success my attire made me a figure of fashion. Now in my dotage it makes me a figure of fun.

LEIGHTON. Certainly not.

VERONICA. Oh, yes. But I shake out my velvet and scent my wrists with French perfume and walk the city's streets at night in memory of the lime light. Do you play an instrument?

LEIGHTON. Sadly, no.

VERONICA. You do sing.

LEIGHTON. No, but I am fond of poetry.

VERONICA. As am I. I must confess I am an old lady in love.

LEIGHTON. If I may be so bold in love with…?

VERONICA. In love with gumballs and licorice sticks. The scent of hyacinth in April, the crunch of fallen leaves under my feet in autumn and the taste of new snow on my tongue.

LEIGHTON. I, too, am in love.

VERONICA. If I may be so bold in love with…?

LEIGHTON. Hot water bottles and black tea. Ragged little boys riding second hand bikes and the forgiving eyes of the very old.

VERONICA. Mercy me, a mystical vision and a miracle on the same day.

LEIGHTON. A miracle?

VERONICA. You've made me feel young again. Perhaps it's time to introduce ourselves.

LEIGHTON. *(rises and bows)* I'm Leighton Tyler. Formerly I taught. Now I warm park benches.

VERONICA. And I am… *(searches in her purse for a card which she offers him)*

LEIGHTON. *(reading the card)* And you are Veronica Wallace, teacher of piano and voice.

VERONICA. Until recently.

LEIGHTON. You've retired?

VERONICA. Not willingly. For years I had my own studio, but at present I find myself in one room without a piano. No matter. This morning I've met a charming bench warmer whom I do hope might become a friend.

LEIGHTON. It will be my pleasure, Miss Veronica, if I may call a new found friend by her first name.

VERONICA. It's been a magical morning, Leighton, if I may call a new found friend by his first name.

(Rises, shakes out her velvet skirt as **THE OLD POOP** *enters.)*

THE OLD POOP. *(shuffling across the stage mumblin')* That ole owl he hoot all night.

VERONICA. Indeed he did.

THE OLD POOP. You heard 'im?

VERONICA. Indeed I did. It gave me the shivers.

LEIGHTON. Miss Veronica, I'd like you to meet the gentleman who cares for the flowers and greenery.

VERONICA. I'm delighted to make your acquaintance.

THE OLD POOP. *(tips his hat)* Much obliged.

VERONICA. Gracious, I must be on my way. *(sways)* I'm a little unsteady after sitting so long. *(to* **THE OLD POOP***)* May I take your arm until we get to the street?

(Embarrassed, **THE OLD POOP** *turns to* **LEIGHTON***, who nods. She takes the old man's arm.)*

We have something in common, you see. I teach music and you tend flowers. A flower is music suffused with color.

THE OLD POOP. You teach music, ma'am?

VERONICA. Until recently.

THE OLD POOP. I got me a granddaughter with the voice of an angel.

VERONICA. *(as they exit)* I would be delighted to meet her.

LEIGHTON. Ah hah!

(Takes a pen and pad from his bag, jots a few notes, tears the sheet from the pad, puts it in his pocket, rises.)

Ah, yes, Miss Veronica it has indeed been a magical morning. *(exits stage right)*

(Brief silence. Music. Brief silence. The season is now fall.)

*(***THE OLD POOP** *enters stage right, shuffles to the coat rack, dons the peaked cap. He takes the orange leaf, attaches it to the bush.)*

THE OLD POOP. Et's October, old friend an' the chill's takin' its tole. That black bird he hoot all night. Warnin' me. Warnin' me t' be ready fer what was comin'.

(**LEIGHTON** *enters stage left wearing his coat, sits on the bench, turns to the old man.*)

LEIGHTON. Hello there.

THE OLD POOP. That ole owl he hoot all night. Come mornin' I'm called t' town where they tells me I'm too old.

LEIGHTON. They?

THE OLD POOP. Town uppity-ups.

LEIGHTON. Oh?

THE OLD POOP. "Don't look good," they says. Old man with mud on his trousers workin' fer the town.

LEIGHTON. Oh, my.

THE OLD POOP. Three weeks they give me.

LEIGHTON. Three weeks?

THE OLD POOP. Three weeks an' I'm gone.

LEIGHTON. But the gardens are beautiful!

THE OLD POOP. Three weeks an' I got me nothin' t' tend.

LEIGHTON. I can't believe it!

THE OLD POOP. Was a time I had me a coin in my pocket, a fish on the hook an' a fiddle at my feet. A time when my back weren't bent an' when I needed socks I bought 'em.

LEIGHTON. I've been told that grand old man, Albert Einstein, strolled the streets of Princeton without socks.

(**HARRIET** *storms on stage left to confront* **LEIGHTON** *wearing a cotton house dress and sweater.*)

HARRIET. Leighton!

LEIGHTON. Harriet? *(Noticing her anger he attempts to deflect it.)* I'm sure you remember the good fellow who tends these gardens.

HARRIET. Yes, we've met.

THE OLD POOP. Aye. Best I find my little one. Tell 'er the news. *(to* **HARRIET***)* You seen a scallywag scootin' down the street, ma'am?

HARRIET. I'm afraid not.

LEIGHTON. Scallywag? Ah! *(slaps his forehead)* Is she the one who lights up a room?

THE OLD POOP. Sets it on fire with her tongue.

LEIGHTON. She's your granddaughter?

THE OLD POOP. Aye. You seen 'er?

LEIGHTON. Yes, indeed! Awhile ago. Down by the newsstand.

THE OLD POOP. Much obliged. *(exits)*

HARRIET. *(to* **LEIGHTON** *)* You bastard!

LEIGHTON. Oh?

HARRIET. I bought that house!

LEIGHTON. I heard.

HARRIET. I must have been out of my mind.

LEIGHTON. About time. How is Jacques adjusting?

HARRIET. He's acclimating. I'm not. And I detest you. Look at me!

LEIGHTON. You're a delight.

HARRIET. In a house dress? I've never in my life worn a house dress!

LEIGHTON. You're no less enticing.

HARRIET. A tenured professor in a house dress?

LEIGHTON. Now you're a house frau as well.

HARRIET. Next thing I know I'll find myself in class wearing an apron! It's more than I can…

(Begins to sob. **LEIGHTON** *rises, takes her in his arms.)*

I'm a professional!

LEIGHTON. You're also a woman, thank God. You look chic in tailored suits and fetching in an apron.

HARRIET. *(pulling away)* I hate you!

LEIGHTON. I was hoping you'd become fond of me.

HARRIET. That would be a miracle!

LEIGHTON. It's rumored I am a miracle man.

HARRIET. You're a devious fruitcake! I'm living alone in a four bedroom house with an arbor needing mending and walls needing paint. And the damn house is haunted. There's a rocking chair by the kitchen window rocking with no one in it! What am I to do?

LEIGHTON. No, what am I to do?

(Lowers her gently to the bench, moves stage left considering her plight, turns.)

First I shall scrub down your big black stove. I assume you have a big black stove that needs scrubbing?

HARRIET. Of course!

LEIGHTON. Next I shall paint your kitchen yellow.

HARRIET. Have you ever painted a wall?

LEIGHTON. No, but I watched my wife paint her toenails. Next I shall mend your arbor.

HARRIET. I assume you have a pair of jeans.

LEIGHTON. No, but I've a pair of nicely mended long johns.

HARRIET. *(springs from the bench)* I can't sit here! I've too much to do! And, Leighton, I can't sleep!

LEIGHTON. *(cupping her face in his hands)* I have a solution for that. A little lovin'.

HARRIET. You're horrible! Joking when I'm losing my sanity!

LEIGHTON. Sanity is sameness. Sameness is comfortable. I've shaken your life a bit. Allow me to shake it a bit more.

HARRIET. God forbid.

LEIGHTON. He gave me the idea. Now listen carefully. What you're to do is get yourself to a beauty salon. Have your hair tinted the color of marmalade and your toenails painted red. I'm taking you to dinner tonight in a very elegant restaurant.

HARRIET. Elegant restaurant? With newspaper in your shoes?

LEIGHTON. I am not a pauper. I fancy the image, but I do have a tie. Tonight you'll not recognize me.

HARRIET. You're serious?

LEIGHTON. I'm serious.

HARRIET. Then tonight you'll not recognize me!

LEIGHTON. And wear a pair of toeless shoes. May I kiss you?

HARRIET. No.

LEIGHTON. Tonight?

HARRIET. You're naughty.

LEIGHTON. But nice. I told little Star I only letch women who take their teeth out at night.

HARRIET. I don't take out my teeth.

LEIGHTON. You're forgiven.

(**STAR** *rushes on stage right. Skids to a stop when she sees them.*)

Ah, Star!

STAR. *(looks around)* I got t' find 'im! *(turns to run off)*

LEIGHTON. No, no, join us, child. I'd like to introduce you to someone.

(**STAR** *turns.*)

Star, this is Miss Gallo. *(to* **HARRIET***)* Harriet, this is my friend, Star.

(**STAR** *turns to* **LEIGHTON**, *who nods. Turns to* **HARRIET**, *hesitates, then recites.*)

STAR. How do you do?

(turns to **LEIGHTON** *who smiles approvingly)*

HARRIET. It's nice to meet you, Star. Who is it you're looking for?

STAR. The old…

LEIGHTON. *(coughs)* Ahem.

STAR. My grandpa.

LEIGHTON. Her grandfather is the caretaker.

HARRIET. Oh?

STAR. Yes, 'um. *(Glances at **LEIGHTON**, who nods.)*

HARRIET. The flowers are lovely.

STAR. *(with a hint of pride.)* He tends 'em.

HARRIET. It seems we have something in common, Star. My grandfather, too, was a man who put seeds in the soil and tended them. You and I are fortunate. I'm happy to have met you. Goodbye, Leighton.

LEIGHTON. Until tonight.

*(**HARRIET** turns to **STAR**, smiles, exits.)*

Miss Gallo is nice, isn't she?

STAR. She's ok.

LEIGHTON. I'm fond of her.

STAR. So?

LEIGHTON. I was hoping you might be fond of her.

STAR. Why?

LEIGHTON. I like my friends to like each other.

STAR. She's your friend?

LEIGHTON. Oh, yes.

STAR. You said I was your friend.

LEIGHTON. You are.

STAR. You got two friends?

LEIGHTON. I have quite a few friends.

STAR. So don't I feel the fool!

LEIGHTON. Why would you feel a fool?

STAR. Doin' those dumb things you taught me!

LEIGHTON. Dumb things?

STAR. *(mimicking herself)* "How do you do?" an' "Yes, 'um!" I learned 'em good, an' then you go an' like her, too! *(runs stage right)*

LEIGHTON. Star?

STAR. *(whirling around)* What?

LEIGHTON. Come back here.

STAR. No!

LEIGHTON. *(softly)* Please come back.

STAR. You just wanna teach me stuff!

LEIGHTON. I'm an old teacher, Star.

STAR. Shine me up 'n show me off!

LEIGHTON. I wanted to…

STAR. I ain't no lady. I'm me!

LEIGHTON. You certainly are. That's why it makes me happy to teach you stuff. Because you're you.

STAR. Like I'm t' believe that?

LEIGHTON. Like you're to believe that. And what makes me happier, Star, is to have you teach me stuff. Stuff. That's a good word. Appropriate. I was a stuffy old professor who thought he knew everything. Since meeting you I find I have a lot to learn. You're my teacher, child. I need you.

STAR. *(near tears)* I gotta find me the old poop.

LEIGHTON. *(gently)* But you'll come again?

(STAR hesitates, nods.)

And why is that?

STAR. Cause you need some teachin'! *(runs off stage right)*

AUDREY. *(from offstage)* Hey! Watch where you're going! *(Enters rubbing her arm.)* Just bumped into that screwy kid.

LEIGHTON. You might be seeing more of her.

AUDREY. Don't spook me.

LEIGHTON. Was she crying?

AUDREY. *(looking up)* No rain so I guess she was crying. *(drops her backpack at **LEIGHTON**'s feet, squats)* I've come to say good-bye.

LEIGHTON. Good-bye comes after hello.

AUDREY. I quit.

LEIGHTON. Quit?

AUDREY. School.

LEIGHTON. Why?

AUDREY. Bored.

LEIGHTON. Boredom is a luxury young people can't afford.

AUDREY. That's what you said.

LEIGHTON. I said?

AUDREY. Yes.

LEIGHTON. When did I say that?

AUDREY. In class. That's why you jumped ship, isn't it? Boredom.

LEIGHTON. No, child.

AUDREY. Oh, come on. You had the guts to do it, so figured I did too. So it was over the walls of ivy to experience real life.

LEIGHTON. And are you?

AUDREY. Experiencing real life? My landlady's kicking me out because I can't pay the rent. As for dining I'm eating peanut butter out of a jar and ripping off fruit stands. If that's real life, hell, yes, I'm experiencing it!

LEIGHTON. Because of me?

AUDREY. You were the inspiration.

LEIGHTON. How are your parents handling this?

AUDREY. Like parents. Cancelled my credit cards. Told me if I don't get back to class I'm on my own.

LEIGHTON. Homeless and hungry.

AUDREY. Poor little me.

LEIGHTON. Before you start sleeping on park benches and kicking empty beer cans in dark alleys would you like a good meal?

AUDREY. Things are looking up.

LEIGHTON. Would you be willing to sweep floors and scrub tubs for room and board?

AUDREY. Like be a maid?

LEIGHTON. Is housework humiliating for someone raised on the right side of the tracks?

AUDREY. Hell, yes!

LEIGHTON. More humiliating than ripping off fruit stands? You say you want to be a writer. Writing is work. Long, hard lonely work. Maybe you should practice working in the real world before you write about it.

AUDREY. You sound like my dad!

LEIGHTON. Dad in absentia.

AUDREY. You just want me to graduate!

LEIGHTON. Yes, and with honors. But first I'd like you to have a good meal. *(reaches into his pocket, removes a slip of newspaper, hands it to her)*

AUDREY. *(reads the slip)* "Help wanted?"

LEIGHTON. Most of us need a little help. This is the address of a house where sauce is simmering on the back burner and spaghetti ready to be put in the pot. Is that your stomach rumbling?

(**AUDREY** *starts to speak.*)

Not a word! Scoot!

(**AUDREY** *grabs her backpack and exits stage right.*)

LEIGHTON. Two birds with one stone. *(rises, stretches, checks his watch)* Tea time… tea and a hot fresh scone! *(twirls, exits Stage Left.)*

(Brief silence. Music. Brief Silence. It is now fall.)

THE OLD POOP. *(enters Stage Right to check on the bush)* Missin' me like I'm missin' you? I ain't forgot ya'. You an' me we go back awhile, don't we? Gettin' chilly, old friend. Goldenrod along the road, last of the apples. Things happenin' so fast makes my head spin. Got me a new job. Think of that. Old man with a new job. An' my little scalllywag, she poundin' away on the piano. And singin'. Praise the Lord she singin' like her ma! *(pats the bush)* I'll be checkin' on ya now an' again. We go back awhile, don't we? We go back ole friend. *(exits)*

LEIGHTON. *(whistling as he enters stage left wearing his old coat and carrying a bag of grapes)* Ah, October's bright blue weather! In little back lanes the fragrance of grapes! *(sinks down on the bench, opens the bag and pops a grape into his mouth)* Last autumn I sat in an office with unwashed windows and a dying pachysandra. Today I sit here watching copper leaves float to my feet. A day for daydreaming.

HARRIET. *(enters stage left wearing her coat)* Leighton?

LEIGHTON. Harriet!

HARRIET. *(with a chuckle)* Same old coat.

LEIGHTON. On the same old fellow.

HARRIET. With the same old moth holes.

LEIGHTON. It's snug.

HARRIET. It's a disgrace.

LEIGHTON. Found it in the attic.

HARRIET. Throw it in the trash.

LEIGHTON. It's the only coat I have.

HARRIET. I'll knit you another.

LEIGHTON. With a drop seat for the potty?

HARRIET. But of course.

LEIGHTON. Then I shall wear it.

HARRIET. What are you doing sitting here?

LEIGHTON. Waiting.

HARRIET. Waiting for what?

LEIGHTON. Waiting for you. *(pats the bench)* Come sit with me.

HARRIET. I haven't time what with school and the house…

LEIGHTON. These grapes are delicious.

HARRIET. I grow my own.

LEIGHTON. I liked you better when you needed a hug.

HARRIET. I didn't say I don't need a hug.

LEIGHTON. Ah, hah!

(digs in his pocket, takes out a scrap of paper, pretends to read it)

This says there's a hugger within walking distance.

(rises, holds out his arms, and she walks into them)

I've missed you.

HARRIET. I've been busy.

LEIGHTON. Too busy to see an old friend?

HARRIET. Too busy planning a supper for Saturday night where I hope to see this old friend.

LEIGHTON. Ah, just you and I?

HARRIET. And a cadre of misfits, I among them, who hang out in my house, thanks to you.

LEIGHTON. Oh?

HARRIET. Since you cast me in the role of earth mother, you devious scoundrel, I have an old poop tending my arbor, a college dropout by the name of Audrey cleaning my toilets, an ancient old woman who swoons on the hour teaching piano in my parlor, and a child with principles feeding my hamster chocolate covered raisons and making him fat! The supper Saturday night is potluck so bring a dish. Your phantom wife is not invited.

LEIGHTON. She isn't fond of Italian.

HARRIET. And we're all painting our toenails.

LEIGHTON. I shall arrive with red toenails, a hunk of Parmesan and a niggling longing to hold you in my arms again.

HARRIET. Niggle away. *(hurries stage left)* And Jacques detests Italian cheese! *(exits)*

LEIGHTON. A party, ah!

*(As he does his little dance **THE OLD POOP** enters stage right.)*

THE OLD POOP. *(examines the bush, mutters)* You doin' fine ole friend. *(turns to **LEIGHTON**)* Good day t' ya.

LEIGHTON. Good day.

THE OLD POOP. That ole owl ain't hootin' of late.

LEIGHTON. Is that right?

THE OLD POOP. Likely catchin' up on his sleep like the rest of us.

LEIGHTON. Likely.

THE OLD POOP. Grannie on my ma's side used to say if you was lookin' out the window come night an' that black bird fly by you was headin' fer heaven soon. Grannie on my pa's side swore an owl egg cure the whoopin' cough.

LEIGHTON. And what do you say?

THE OLD POOP. I say t'is time t' pick the grapes, bale the hay an' let the kiddies paint the pumpkins. Good day t' you. *(exits)*

LEIGHTON. *(Chuckles, moves downstage to speak to the audience as he did at the opening of the play. Pointing a thumb toward the coat he wears.)* This coat? Yes, the same old coat. Fine wool. As I told you my great-great grandfather wore this coat during the dark days of the depression. One does not throw out a serviceable coat, does one? No, no. Back at the University they still delight in telling tales about the ragged old professor with newspaper in his shoes, and rumors still abound. But as for the rumor that the ragged old simpleton is performing miracles? Ridiculous. *(winks at the audience, exits whistling)*

The End

STAGE SETTING

On stage as the play opens: A bright green park bench just right of center, a dark green wooden coat rack up left and a six foot cardboard cutout of a large bush stage right. Three hats hang on the coat rack, a dark woolen hat, a misshapen straw hat and a faded yellow peaked hat. Also hanging on the coat rack are three large cardboard cutouts to be hung on the bush during the play, a bright green leaf, a pink flower and an orange leaf. Both the hats and the color of the leaves indicate a change of season.

PROPERTY PLOT

LEIGHTON carries a dark tote bag containing a paper bag from which characters mime eating grapes, several newspaper clippings and a pad and pen.

HARRIET carries a leather brief case.

AUDREY carries a back pack.

VERONICA carries a draw-string purse in which is a dainty handkerchief and a business card.

COSTUME PLOT

During the course of the play characters move through three seasons. Minimal costume changes indicate each season.

LEIGHTON. As the play opens he wears a camel's hair coat *(or similar coat)* marred by moth holes. Under the coat he wears a colorful Hawaiian shirt in which he appears in the summer scene. He wears the coat again in the autumn scene.

HARRIET. Enters wearing an attractive top coat over a pretty house dress in which she appears in the summer scene. The top coat is again worn in the autumn scene.

STAR. Wears yellow overalls found in a used clothing bin and run down sneakers without socks. The overalls are a bit short as she has outgrown them.

OLD POOP. Wears old dark trousers and work boots. He dons the woolen cap in the winter scene, the straw hat in the summer scene and the peaked cap in autumn.

VERONICA. Wears an ancient green velvet gown.

ONCE AGAIN IN GLYN KERRIE

**A DRAMATIC COMEDY
IN ONE ACT**

CHARACTERS

CORDELIA – A woman of eighty three.
YOUNG CORDELIA – Cordelia as a child and young woman.
PAPA – Her father.
MAMA – Her mother.
WILL – Her teenage love and husband.

SCENE

The action takes place at a bus stop.

TIME

The present.

(AT RISE: On an otherwise bare stage four white stools sit slightly upstage left and a bench and sign announcing "BUS STOP" downstage right. The bench and sign are painted a deep maroon.)

(As the play opens **PAPA**, **MAMA**, **WILL** *and* **YOUNG CORDELIA**, *enter stage left to sit on the stools.* **MAMA** *and* **YOUNG CORDELIA** *are dressed in white,* **MAMA** *with a red flowered apron,* **YOUNG CORDELIA** *with a red ribbon in her long hair.* **PAPA** *and* **WILL** *wear light beige shirts and trousers,* **PAPA** *with a red tie,* **WILL** *with a red cardigan sweater. They live in the memory of the main character,* **CORDELIA**, *who after a moment enters downstage right carrying a small suitcase and a cat carrier.)*

CORDELIA. *(sets the suitcase and carrier by the bench, peers off stage left, turns to the audience)* Good morning. *(checks her watch)* And it is a good morning. The bus should be along shortly. I expect we'll be riding together. Cordelia's my name. No, no, not Cornelia, Cordelia. Yes. I've lived in that retirement home across the way for a number of years. Pleasant? For most I expect. Unfortunately, or perhaps fortunately, I was not like the others. The only liberal in a hot bed of conservatism, or the only conservative in a hot bed of liberals. Take your pick. But I was different. Perhaps we all are. I'm 83 years old, paint with oils, drive a jeep, cut my own toenails and have never worn a pant suit. *(adjusts her jacket)* My jacket? Too large, yes. We shrink as we age. I expect I'm almost the size of the child I was. This morning I'm returning to where I was that child. I'm going home.

YOUNG CORDELIA. *(runs to* **CORDELIA**, *tugs on her sleeve)* You say we're going home?

CORDELIA. Yes, child.

YOUNG CORDELIA. Yippee!

(twirls happily calling to those on the stools, hereafter referred to as **THE OTHERS***)*

We're going home!

THE OTHERS. *(From the stools they speak softly, sounding almost ghostlike.)* Yippee!

CORDELIA. *(to the audience)* Home to marmalade on the kitchen table, Papa in the breakfast nook eating scrambled eggs and scrapple and...

YOUNG CORDELIA. And Jenny wren singing in her nest by the kitchen door!

CORDELIA. Home to Mama shelling peas in the garden, water spilling over the edge of the old stone bird bath during a summer storm and...

YOUNG CORDELIA. And bare feet squishing in puddles of mud.

CORDELIA. To palatine light on green grass and the whispers and laughter of childhood. *(peers stage left, checks her watch)* The bus is late.

YOUNG CORDELIA. *(calling to* **THE OTHERS***)* The bus is late!

THE OTHERS. *(softly)* Late...late...

CORDELIA. *(lifts a hand to her mouth, slaps it down with her other hand)* Dreadful! A woman my age biting her nails! In truth I'm a bit uneasy, but they won't discover I'm missing until teatime. Surely the bus will be here soon. *(sighs)* Waiting and watching. Women my age have been faithful custodians of uneasy waiting and watching. Waiting at bedsides and through long winters of grief. Watching at sunrise for the miracle of birth and at sunset for departures. And today I find myself waiting for a bus which will carry me home to weathered farm wagons, white horses on hills and old taverns with signs saying, "Welcome."

YOUNG CORDELIA. To swing on the lowest branch of Grandma's magnolia tree again!

THE OTHERS. *(softly)* Magnolia tree…magnolia tree…

CORDELIA. And taste raw honey on the tip of my tongue.

YOUNG CORDELIA. On the tip of my tongue.

THE OTHERS. *(softly)* On the tip of my tongue…

YOUNG CORDELIA. And steal cream from the top of the milk bottle and feed stray kittens!

CORDELIA. Yes, child, yes, back in Glyn Kerrie.

YOUNG CORDELIA. *(twirls, calling to* **THE OTHERS***)* Back in Glyn Kerrie!

THE OTHERS. *(ghostlike)* Glyn Kerrie…Glyn Kerrie

CORDELIA. *(bends down to straighten her bags, turns to the audience)* This carrier? For pets, of course. Mitzi, a cat and Jiggs, a fox terrier. Together again. Returning to the home where they raised me. To where wooden screen doors swung back and forth on summer afternoons. Where a bowl of roses sat in the parlor, peach ice cream waited in the churn and the table was spread with a lace cloth for Sunday supper. To where the milkman set a bottle of milk on the stoop before sunrise and the eggman a basket of brown eggs on the kitchen table at noon.

YOUNG CORDELIA. To where Papa said grace and Mama made me chew everything twenty times and when she wasn't looking I used a piece of bread to push peas onto my fork!

(She skips upstage and around the stools singing from the childhood song, "Here we go round the mulberry bush, the mulberry bush, the mulberry bush"…)

CORDELIA. *(She joins in softly.)* "Here we go round the Mulberry bush so early in the morning." *(turns to the audience, gesturing toward the stools)* The others? They'll ride along with me, of course. They're always with me. One can leave home with a hug, a tear, a promise to write, or one can slam the door and run to the ends of the earth. But we cannot outrun our memories. They're always with us, and they, too, are heading home. Where is that bus?

YOUNG CORDELIA. Where is that bus?

CORDELIA. When I don't appear at tea time they'll check my room, When they don't find me in my room they'll think I might be asleep in the library, and when they don't find me asleep in the library they'll imagine I'm skulking in the halls. Skulking. Isn't that a delicious word? I don't recall ever having skulked, but might take it up someday. Where is that dratted bus?

YOUNG CORDELIA. I can't see it!

MAMA. *(moving swiftly into the scene)* How do you expect to see anything clearly when you're not wearing your glasses!

CORDELIA. *(to the audience)* I was fitted for glasses when I was eight and I did hate wearing them.

YOUNG CORDELIA. No one else wears glasses! All the kids laugh at me! *(runs stage right)*

MAMA. Cordelia, come back here.

YOUNG CORDELIA. I'll be late for school!

MAMA. Stop this minute.

YOUNG CORDELIA. *(stands with head down)* Gee whiz!

MAMA. Did you break your glasses?

YOUNG CORDELIA. No.

MAMA. Where are they?

YOUNG CORDELIA. In my pocket.

MAMA. Put them on.

YOUNG CORDELIA. Gee whiz.

MAMA. If you don't wear your glasses you won't see what's written on the blackboard.

YOUNG CORDELIA. Dumb old glasses.

MAMA. If you can't see what's written on the blackboard you won't pass your spelling test. And if you don't pass your spelling test you won't be promoted to fourth grade.

YOUNG CORDELIA. My dumb old glasses make me look like a toad. *(sniffles)*

MAMA. Nonsense.

YOUNG CORDELIA. Dumb old Willie Barlow said I look like a toad!

MAMA. Nonsense.

(**PAPA** *moves swiftly to join them.*)

YOUNG CORDELIA. Papa!

PAPA. What's up?

YOUNG CORDELIA. Mama's making me wear my glasses!

PAPA. It's rumored glasses are meant to be worn.

YOUNG CORDELIA. I hate them!

PAPA. Have you noticed Papa wears spectacles?

YOUNG CORDELIA. But you're a papa.

PAPA. Do you think Willy Barlow would tell your papa he looks like a toad?

YOUNG CORDELIA. A papa is different.

PAPA. So is my little girl. My Cordelia can see what classmates can't unless they're wearing magical spectacles.

YOUNG CORDELIA. *(taking her glasses from her pocket)* These aren't magical.

PAPA. Do you think Papa would buy spectacles for his Cordelia if they weren't magical? Let's think about this. *(to* **MAMA***)* Shall we think about this, Mama?

MAMA. That would be best.

PAPA. *(to* **YOUNG CORDELIA***)* Does Willy Barlow wear spectacles?

YOUNG CORDELIA. No.

PAPA. Do other children in your class wear spectacles?

YOUNG CORDELIA. No.

PAPA. That's sad, isn't it, Mama?

MAMA. It does seem sad.

PAPA. Put on your spectacles, sugar plum.

YOUNG CORDELIA. Gee whiz.

PAPA. You and I are taking a walk.

(Holds out his hand, she hesitates, puts on her glasses, takes his hand, they walk stage left. **PAPA** *stops.)*

Look!

YOUNG CORDELIA. What?

PAPA. Diamonds!

YOUNG CORDELIA. Diamonds?

PAPA. *(crouches and points)* See how the dew on that little leaf sparkles as it reaches up to catch a sunbeam?

YOUNG CORDELIA. Ooh...

PAPA. It sparkles like the little diamond in Mama's wedding band. Do you think Willy Barlow knows that overnight the Good Lord sprinkles farmers' fields with diamonds?

YOUNG CORDELIA. Bet he doesn't.

PAPA. Because he not wearing magical spectacles. Poor Willy Barlow.

YOUNG CORDELIA. *(giggles)* Poor Willy Barlow.

PAPA. *(rising)* And look, little one.

YOUNG CORDELIA. What, Papa?

PAPA. *(pointing)* On the fence.

YOUNG CORDELIA. What?

PAPA. A spider web. While we were sleeping a little gray spider spent most of the night weaving this web. Look closely. Isn't it lovely? That little spider has woven a web as soft and intricate as the shawl Santa gave mama last Christmas.

YOUNG CORDELIA. Can we come out some night and watch a little gray spider weave a web?

PAPA. It only happens in the dark. I don't know if we could see him.

YOUNG CORDELIA. Then how can he see to weave his web?

PAPA. I've wondered about that since I was your age and I've concluded spiders wear magical spectacles.

YOUNG CORDELIA. I'm going to tell Willy Barlow he doesn't see what I see because he doesn't wear glasses!

(**PAPA** *chuckles, pats her head, returns to his stool.*)

CORDELIA. *(to the audience)* Why don't I remember rainy days? Why don't I remember the depression when food was scarce and homeless men sat on the kitchen porch while Mama fed them hot pea soup? Why don't I remember the day Papa slammed the door and Mama's tears fell into the dishpan? I suspect we put on magical spectacles in old age.

YOUNG CORDELIA. *(Eyes closed and smiling she sways as she sings, "Here we go round the mulberry bush, the mulberry bush, the mulberry bush...")*

CORDELIA. And around the mulberry bush I went. My first two-wheeler, my first blemish, my first bra, my first party when we put a record on the Victrola and I danced with a boy. Childhood wrapped in tissue and tied with a bow.

YOUNG CORDELIA. *(calls in a hushed voice)* Mama, wake up! It's my birthday!

CORDELIA. My birthday?

YOUNG CORDELIA. Mama, I'm thirteen!

CORDELIA. *(to the audience)* Thirteen.

YOUNG CORDELIA. Today's my birthday, mama. I'm a teenager!

MAMA. *(stumbles Downstage rubbing her eyes)* Happy birthday, sweetheart.

YOUNG CORDELIA. When may I open my present?

MAMA. After I wash up.

YOUNG CORDELIA. At breakfast?

MAMA. At breakfast.

(**MAMA** and **YOUNG CORDELIA** *lower their heads and stand quietly.*)

CORDELIA. It was so hard to wait. It's always so hard to wait when something good is going to happen. Now where is that bus?

YOUNG CORDELIA. *(raising her head)* Now, Mama?

MAMA. *(raising her head)* We'll wait for Papa. I hear him in the hall.

PAPA. *(hugging **YOUNG CORDELIA**)* Happy birthday, young lady. *(sniffs)* Ah, pancakes! Shall we sit down?

(They mime sitting at the table, bowing their heads.)

Thank you, Lord, for our birthday girl, a blessing to her mama and me. And, oh, yes, thank you for pancakes!

MAMA. You may open your present now, Cordelia.

YOUNG CORDELIA. *(mimes opening a package)* A bracelet!

MAMA. I told Papa every young lady should have a charm bracelet.

PAPA. A gold bracelet, Mama said.

YOUNG CORDELIA. *(awed)* Is it real gold?

PAPA. Real gold. Check your first charm.

MAMA. Papa chose it.

YOUNG CORDELIA. A heart!

MAMA. What's written on it?

YOUNG CORDELIA. *(reads)* "Love."

CORDELIA. *(softly)* Love.

PAPA. A reminder that down the road one thing that can never be taken from us is love given and love received.

YOUNG CORDELIA. *(near tears)* Papa…Mama…this is the best birthday ever.

(They link arms and return to their stools.)

CORDELIA. And three years later…

YOUNG CORDELIA. *(from her stool)* Wake up, Mama, it's my birthday. *(slides off her stool)* I'm sixteen!

MAMA. *(slides off her stool rubbing her eyes)* Up so early?

YOUNG CORDELIA. You said there's to be a surprise.

MAMA. We'd best wake, Papa.

(*Taking* **YOUNG CORDELIA**'s *arm, they walk downstage.*)

YOUNG CORDELIA. (*calls*) Papa!

PAPA. (*joining them*) Ready for an adventure?

YOUNG CORDELIA. I couldn't sleep!

PAPA. Tell your mother to put on her white gloves we're going into town!

YOUNG CORDELIA. Why are we going into town?

PAPA. (*turns to* **MAMA**) Why are we going into town, Mama?

MAMA. We're going into town to have Cordelia fitted for contract lenses, papa.

PAPA. (*to* **CORDELIA**) No more spectacles!

YOUNG CORDELIA. No more spectacles?

PAPA. And woe to Billy Barlow! Woe to all the lads who will lose their hearts to our birthday girl!

PAPA & YOUNG CORDELIA. Woe to Billy Barlow!

(**MAMA** *and* **PAPA** *step back and lower their heads.*)

CORDELIA. And woe to me a year later when I lost my heart to Billy Barlow.

WILL. (*enters the scene*) Cordy?

YOUNG CORDELIA. (*turns*) Will?

WILL. (*mimes handing her a small box*) Happy Birthday.

YOUNG CORDELIA. Thank you. (*mimes opening the box*) Ooh…

WILL. Read what's written on it.

YOUNG CORDELIA. (*reads silently*) Oh, Will…!

(**WILL** *leans down, gives her a quick kiss on the cheek, steps back and lowers his head as* **MAMA** *enters the scene.*)

YOUNG CORDELIA. (*showing her present to* **MAMA**) A birthday present from Will, mama!

MAMA. Very pretty but…but it isn't gold.

CORDELIA. (*to the audience*) Gold was expensive.

YOUNG CORDELIA. Gold is expensive.

MAMA. Indeed.

YOUNG CORDELIA. It's sterling silver.

MAMA. And your bracelet is gold.

YOUNG CORDELIA. He saved all year!

MAMA. A thoughtful young man.

YOUNG CORDELIA. And it's a heart!

MAMA. Nevertheless…

YOUNG CORDELIA. I want it on my bracelet!

MAMA. *(studying the charm)* Papa would not approve of what is written on it.

(Mimes reading as **WILL**, *still slightly removed from the scene, speaks.)*

WILL. To Cordy, love, Will.

PAPA. *(moves forward angrily)* He's too young to be saying such things!

YOUNG CORDELIA. He'll be eighteen in April.

WILL. Come April I'll be eighteen.

PAPA. Still a young pup. Let him grow up, hold a job.

YOUNG CORDELIA. He mops the floor in the grocery!

WILL. And I stack the shelves.

PAPA. Makes a dollar here and there, yes, I'll give him that. But not enough to buy our girl a gold charm. Love? Nonsense!

MAMA. Were you a young pup when you were eighteen?

PAPA. I was a damn fool doing damn fool things with the other young pups on campus!

MAMA. I still have the note you wrote when you left for school saying you loved me, asking me to wait. Well, I waited and I wouldn't have waited for a fool.

PAPA. You still have that note?

MAMA. I cherish that note. *(turns to her daughter)* We'll have the jeweler attach William's heart to your charm bracelet.

YOUNG CORDELIA. Oh, Mama, thank you.

CORDELIA. *(softly)* Thank you, Mama.

PAPA. *(shaking his head, mutters)* Still has that damn fool note.

MAMA. And I still have that damn fool husband.

PAPA. *(embracing* **MAMA***, looks over her shoulder the tell his daughter)* Sure you want that young pup's heart on your bracelet?

YOUNG CORDELIA. I'm sure, Papa!

*(***PAPA*** and ***MAMA*** *return to their stools holding hands.)*

CORDELIA. I was a senior in high school when Will came home on his Christmas break.

WILL. *(Singing "Jingle Bells" he moves to stand behind* **YOUNG CORDELIA.***)* Merry Christmas, Cordy.

YOUNG CORDELIA. *(spinning around)* Will! You're home!

WILL. I'm home! *(hugs her)*

CORDELIA. And his first night home...

WILL. *(mimes holding a something in his hand)* Just one.

YOUNG CORDELIA. No.

WILL. A sip?

YOUNG CORDELIA. No.

WILL. Just a sip?

YOUNG CORDELIA. No.

WILL. Lots of girls do.

YOUNG CORDELIA. Do not.

WILL. Do at school.

YOUNG CORDELIA. Don't in Glyn Kerrie.

WILL. Yeah, Glyn Kerrie, where you can't have fun.

YOUNG CORDELIA. We have fun.

WILL. Not like at school.

YOUNG CORDELIA. So go back to school.

WILL. Come on. Just a taste.

YOUNG CORDELIA. "Lips that taste liquor shall never touch mine!"

CORDELIA. Did I really say that?

WILL. Gonna start bashing bottles in bars?

YOUNG CORDELIA. I hate you!

WILL. Didn't know you were a goody-goody.

YOUNG CORDELIA. Didn't know you liked fast girls! *(starts upstage.)*

WILL. Cordy, wait! Look, I'm pouring it out. *(She turns. He mimes pouring beer on the ground.)* See? Now may I?

YOUNG CORDELIA. May you what?

WILL. You know.

YOUNG CORDELIA. No, I don't.

WILL. Yes, you do. You do, don't you?

YOUNG CORDELIA. Maybe.

WILL. Maybe yes, or maybe no?

YOUNG CORDELIA. Maybe…yes. *(closes her eyes, purses her lips)*

WILL. *(kisses her chastely)* That means you're my sweetheart, right?

YOUNG CORDELIA. Guess so.

WILL. And you'll wait for me like your mama waited?

YOUNG CORDELIA. Guess so. *(teasing)* Since I can't have any fun in old Glyn Kerrie anyway.

CORDELIA. The week Will graduated college papa announced our engagement. The week I graduated art school Papa walked me down the aisle. And the week after Papa walked me down the aisle we kicked the dirt of old Glyn Kerrie off our boots and headed for the city.

*(**YOUNG CORDELIA** and **WILL** mime rocking to the movement of a train as **MAMA** and **PAPA** move stage center.)*

YOUNG CORDELIA. *(as if looking out a train window calls)* Goodbye, Mama, goodbye, Papa.

CORDELIA. *(softly)* Goodbye, Mama. Goodby, Papa.

MAMA & PAPA. *(waving)* Goodbye, goodbye.

(They return to their stools.)

(YOUNG CORDELIA and WILL walk stage left, turn, gaze out over the heads of the audience in awe.)

WILL. The buildings so tall! A city lit all night!

YOUNG CORDELIA. So many people!

WILL. Taxi cabs and automobiles!

YOUNG CORDELIA. I'm going to paint everything I see.

WILL. And when I finish law school I'll be…

CORDELIA. The best lawyer in the city!

WILL. The best damn lawyer in the city!

YOUNG CORDELIA. Will, you're swearing!

WILL. That's what men do in the city! And women drink wine! So maybe you'll take a sip.

YOUNG CORDELIA. Maybe.

WILL. *(mimes tossing his hat into the air)* Life here we come!

CORDELIA. Innocents in the big city that first summer. Together we dipped our toes in the rough surf of the Atlantic Ocean for the first time.

YOUNG CORDELIA. *(hopping back)* It's so cold!

WILL. I'll warm you up. *(mimes splashing water on her)*

YOUNG CORDELIA. *(squeals)* Ooh!

CORDELIA. Together we ate our first lobster, saw our first play, wandered through the zoo.

YOUNG CORDELIA. I want to see an elephant.

WILL. And a gorilla.

YOUNG CORDELIA. And bears.

CORDELIA. We wanted to see everything.

YOUNG CORDELIA. Churches with stained glass windows, babies with nannies, children wearing braces!

WILL. Women wearing pants!

CORDELIA. We saw our first museum, our first art gallery and rode our first subway. It was magical.

YOUNG CORDELIA. Oh, Will, it's magical!

CORDELIA. But when gray December shrouded the bright lights and I trudged up three flights of stairs to a cold apartment we had our first fight.

WILL. *(moving his stool downstage, he sits to mime writing)* No.

YOUNG CORDELIA. Why?

WILL. You know why.

YOUNG CORDELIA. We never do.

WILL. We will.

YOUNG CORDELIA. When?

WILL. Soon.

YOUNG CORDELIA. Why are you always working?

WILL. We can't live on love.

YOUNG CORDELIA. I don't think you still love me.

WILL. Of course I still love you.

YOUNG CORDELIA. *(rubbing her hands to warm them)* Then turn up the heat!

WILL. We can't afford to turn up the heat.

YOUNG CORDELIA. Then let's go out and buy roasted chestnuts. Or let's go out and look at Christmas decorations in store windows. Or at least let's turn up the heat, and put a record on the Victrola and dance.

WILL. I have a test tomorrow.

YOUNG CORDELIA. *(near tears)* I want to go home!

WILL. You are home.

YOUNG CORDELIA. I'm not home! I'm not home! I want to go home!

CORDELIA. Home to where when icicles hung from the eves, Papa lit the logs in the fireplace, and mama made a pots of pea soup.

YOUNG CORDELIA. Home to Glyn Kerrie!

WILL. Cordy, you're with me. When you're with me and I'm with you we're home.

YOUNG CORDELIA. If we were really home we would be warming our hands around a cup of mama's green pea soup!

WILL. We'll have pea soup tomorrow in the automat.

YOUNG CORDELIA. You can't get pea soup in the automat!

WILL. Bet you can!

YOUNG CORDELIA. Bet you can't!

WILL. So ok!

YOUNG CORDELIA. Ok!

WILL. I can't study with you bitching! I work so I can finish school and afford to feed us!

CORDELIA. Will walked out and slammed the door. And my tears fell into the dishpan. But before long a leafy green spring crept into the city unannounced.

YOUNG CORDELIA. *(mimes carrying an armful of flowers)* Daffodils, Will, from the market! Let me find a jar to put them in! They'll brighten up the whole room! And *(twirling joyously)* you've turned up the heat!

WILL. Exams are over, I'm graduating in June and a law firm is sniffing around!

(raising their arms in triumph they take a few steps upstage, stand with backs to the audience)

CORDELIA. That fall Will was working for a fine law firm and I'd sold my first painting. We found a nice apartment, hung a bird feeder at the window, ate roasted chestnuts on the street again. We were young and life was wondrous. Soon I would hang a third heart on my gold charm bracelet.

PAPA. *(rushes downstage, mimes answering the phone)* Hello? What? Who? *(gasps)* Praise the Lord! *(calls)* Mama?

MAMA. *(rising from her stool)* Yes?

PAPA. Phone!

MAMA. What?

PAPA. Telephone!

MAMA. Who is it?

PAPA. Cordelia!

MAMA. Who?

PAPA. *(mumbles)* Deafer by the day. *(shouts)* Cordelia!

MAMA. *(rushing forward)* Is everything alright?

PAPA. Better than alright! *(into the phone)* Here's Mama! *(hands the phone to* **MAMA***)*

MAMA. What, dear? Please talk louder.

PAPA. *(grabs the phone)* Gotta talk louder. Mama lost her hearing aid. *(hands phone to* **MAMA***)*

MAMA. A baby? *(to* **PAPA***)* A baby! *(into the phone)* Oh, sweetheart, how wonderful! *(to* **PAPA***)* You're going to be a grandpa!

PAPA. And you're going to be a grandma!

MAMA. *(weeping)* Praise the Lord!

CORDELIA. *(softly)* While Mama praised the Lord, Will and I waited. And in nine months…

MAMA. *(rushing to the phone)* Cordelia? Oh, Cordelia! *(calls)* Papa?

PAPA. What?

MAMA. Phone!

PAPA. Who is it?

MAMA. Cordelia!

PAPA. Who?

MAMA. *(mumbles)* Deafer by the day. *(shouts)* Cordelia!

PAPA. *(rushes forward)* Everything alright?

MAMA. *(to* **CORDELIA***)* Now talk louder, dear, Papa lost his hearing aid. *(hands the phone to* **PAPA***)*

PAPA. A girl? *(to* **MAMA***)* Mama, it's a girl! *(into the phone)* Red hair? *(to* **MAMA***)* We got ourselves a redhead, mama!

MAMA. What's her name?

PAPA. *(into the phone)* What's her name? *(to* **MAMA***)* Name's Gretchen! We got ourselves a little redhead by the name of Gretchen!

MAMA. Tell her to send photographs.

PAPA. Send photos, lots and lots of photos, and keep 'em coming!

CORDELIA. So into the mailbox they went. Back to Glyn Kerrie. Lot and lots of photos.

MAMA. *(mimes looking at a photo)* Gretchen in her baby carriage.

PAPA. *(looking over MAMA's shoulder)* Pretty as a picture!

MAMA. *(a photo)* Gretchen all dressed up for her first day in kindergarten!

CORDELIA. In the dress you made, Mama.

PAPA. Pretty as a picture!

MAMA. *(a photo)* Her dance recital!

PAPA. Just eight years old and…

MAMA & PAPA. *(laughing)* Pretty as a picture!

PAPA. Pretty as a picture.

MAMA. *(a photo)* Sixth grade! My goodness!

PAPA. *(a photo)* High school? Can't believe it, Mama. Our little Gretchen in high school! That one's going to set the world a-fire.

(**PAPA** and **MAMA** *turn from the audience. After a count of four they turn back.*)

MAMA. The phone's ringing, Papa, get the phone.

PAPA. *(into the phone)* Hello? *(to MAMA)* It's Cordelia. *(into the phone)* What is it, sweetheart, talk louder. What? Oh, dear God…

MAMA. Polio? Poliomyelitis? *(screams)* No!

PAPA. *(into the receiver)* Bring her home, honey. We'll take care of her. Take care of you both.

CORDELIA. So we did. We took our Gretchen home to Glyn Kerrie where she rests beneath a weeping willow which shed its tears with us.

(**ALL** *stand motionless. At the count of four* **YOUNG CORDELIA** *sinks to her knees, her hair sweeping the floor.*)

CORDELIA. *(head lifted, eyes closed)* One month, six months, a year.

(*As* **MAMA** *and* **PAPA** *return to their stool* **WILL** *takes a handkerchief from his pocket, wipes his eyes, raises* **YOUNG CORDELIA** *gently to her feet, embraces her.*)

WILL. Spring again, sweetheart. *(points)* Lilacs, from the market.

YOUNG CORDELIA. *(Moves slowly across the stage as if in a trance, mimes burying her face in lilacs. Turns to* **WILL.***)* Lilacs in the city.

WILL. Lilacs in the city for my love.

YOUNG CORDELIA. Are there places in the city where lilacs actually grow?

WILL. Probably.

YOUNG CORDELIA. I'm going to look. I'm going to look for lilacs blooming in some abandoned patch.

WILL. If you look, Cordy, you'll find them.

YOUNG CORDELIA. Find them and photograph them. And I'll find an old stone bird bath.

WILL. In the rain.

CORDELIA. And an old woman planting petunias.

YOUNG CORDELIA. And an old man whittling.

WILL. *(laughing)* I doubt that.

CORDELIA. But I found him.

YOUNG CORDELIA. Found him and photographed him!

CORDELIA. I found a grape arbor behind a shed.

YOUNG CORDELIA. And blue wild flowers in an alley.

CORDELIA. Country life in a teeming city! Photographs to soothe the hearts of those who long for the sun-lit fields of their childhood

(Both she and **YOUNG CORDELIA** *mime studying their bracelet.)*

The third heart on my bracelet was given me by Will when Gretchen was born. It reads…

YOUNG CORDELIA. *(reads)* "For Gretchen, with love."

CORDELIA. And the fourth and final heart on my bracelet reads…

YOUNG CORDELIA. *(reads)* "From Gretchen, with love."

(Both stand quietly a moment.)

CORDELIA. *(steps forward, peers down the road)* Where is that dratted bus? *(after a moment turns to the audience)* A gift given by a country childhood is often hard won integrity. Will and I did our best to tender that integrity, but I worry we might have sold it now and then on our way to the top for seven pieces of silver.

YOUNG CORDELIA. Papa, the web!

PAPA. *(a ghost-like voice from the rear)* Careful, Cordelia, we mustn't shatter the web.

YOUNG CORDELIA. We mustn't shatter the web!

CORDELIA. How many delicately woven webs of other artist's dreams have I shattered finagling to have my photographs hung in the perfect space in the perfect uptown gallery?

WILL. *(ghost-like voice from the rear)* Don't we have to give a little, take a little, Cordy?

CORDELIA. Did we give too little, take too much?

MAMA. *(ghost-like voice from the rear)* You were good children.

CORDELIA. Mama?

MAMA. Yes, dear?

CORDELIA. I wish you'd be waiting on the corner when my bus arrives.

MAMA. What makes you think I won't be?

CORDELIA. But Mama, you, and Daddy, and Gretchen and Will, you're all…

MAMA. Just resting beneath the weeping willow? Sometimes, child, you take too much for granted and sometimes you take too little.

CORDELIA. Do I take too little?

YOUNG CORDELIA. Yep. *(skips to stand beside those sitting on stools, heads lowered)*

CORDELIA. *(to the audience)* When I'm once again in Glyn Kerrie, I shall spend my mornings making pots of pea soup for church suppers and my evenings wandering the thickets in my nightgown to watch a little gray spiders spin his web. But only after tossing my contact lenses in the trash and putting on my magical spectacles. So they may make me look like a frog. I don't give a damn. *(peering stage left)* Oh! Here comes the bus!

The End

COSTUME PLOT

CORDELIA wears a well tailored maroon suit, black leather shoes, gloves and handbag.

YOUNG CORDELIA wears a pale pink blouse and deep pink flowered skirt.

THE OTHERS: Those on stools, loved ones remembered, are dressed in gray or white.

PAPA wears gray trousers and dress shirt and a maroon tie.

MAMA wears a white skirt and blouse with a maroon flowered apron.

WILL wears dark gray pants, pale gray shirt and a maroon cardigan.

PROPERTY PLOT

Personal properties are mimed. This, of course, is at the desecration of the director.

SET PLOT

The stage is empty but for three white stools up stage left and a sign reading "BUS STOP" down stage left.

Also by
Jean Lenox Toddie...

A Little Something for the Ducks

And Go To Innisfree

And Send Forth a Raven

By the Name of Kensington

Is that the Bus to Pittsburgh?

The Juice of Wild Strawberries

**Late Sunday Afternoon,
Early Sunday Evening**

Looking for a Better Berry Bush

Rockin' on the Milky Way

Scent of Honeysuckle

The Silver Apples of the Moon

**Tell Me Another Story,
Sing Me a Song**

Those Singing Sunday Mornings

White Room of My Remembering

Please visit our website **samuelfrench.com** for complete descriptions and licensing information.

OTHER TITLES AVAILABLE FROM SAMUEL FRENCH

ROCKIN' ON THE MILKY WAY

Jean Lenox Toddie

Collection of One-Act plays / 3m, 7f / Simple Sets

Rockin' On The Milky Way is a collection of three one-act plays entitled *Moon Beams In Mid-Morning, One White Winter Night* and *I Remember Heaven, Of Course.* These plays by internationally known playwright, Jean Lenox Toddie, treat the audience to an evening of comedy and drama that celebrates life, love and the tangled relationships of lovers and families. A rocking chair sits center stage in each play. Ten colorful characters range from a middle-age woman sitting in the Florida Everglades with a shot gun across her lap, to a charming male poet who dines on candied locusts and marinated artichoke hearts, to a lovely young mute singing her own soundless song, to a quirky old lady booted out of heaven for bad behavior.

SAMUELFRENCH.COM

OTHER TITLES AVAILABLE FROM SAMUEL FRENCH

THOSE SINGING SUNDAY MORNINGS

Jean Lenox Toddie

Dramatic Comedy / 2f / Simple set

An artist who dwells in a tree house is heading out to play poker in Peru with a monkey on her shoulder. Her niece wants to drop out of high school and see the world with her. Are they looking for adventure or running away? Will dipping their toes in lotus ponds in Japan, eating raw eggs in the hills of Eastern Europe and seeking the wee wild ones who dance in the woods of Ireland at the full moon heal these hearts? Laughter, tears and unanswered questions fill the backpacks of these wanderers - if they are allowed to leave.

OTHER TITLES AVAILABLE FROM SAMUEL FRENCH

AND GO TO INNISFREE

Jean Lenox Toddie

Dramatic Comedy / 3f / Bare stage

It's October. The beach is deserted. A woman appears, flowered parasol raised and long skirt sweeping the sand. She has come to make a decision, but will she make it alone? The middle aged matron she was argues for the comfort of a retirement home. The child she was urges her to sit again and eat blackberries, to lie under the brambles and study ants, and to arise at long last and go to Innisfree.

SAMUELFRENCH.COM

OTHER TITLES AVAILABLE FROM SAMUEL FRENCH

THE JUICE OF WILD STRAWBERRIES

Jean Lenox Toddie

Comic Drama / 1m, 1f

A woman seeks renewal after loss in this touching 35 minute play. Ellie, who has lived on land "flat as an old man's feet" for forty years, packs a satchel, covers the sofa with a sheet and sets out to see what's on the other side of the mountain. She is followed. Is it Calvin there behind her, or is it her husband? "This gem celebrates life, love and the wisdom that comes with age." Mill Mountain Theatre, Roanoke, VA.

SAMUELFRENCH.COM

www.ingramcontent.com/pod-product-compliance
Lightning Source LLC
Chambersburg PA
CBHW070648300426
44111CB00013B/2332